From Pings to Purchases: WhatsApp Strategies for Digital Marketers

For that hustling marketer who's optimized every ad and email but hasn't unlocked the power of the inbox that's always open.

Published by Aries Ram

This book is for informational purposes only. The author and publisher have made every effort to ensure accuracy, but they assume no responsibility for errors or omissions. The strategies and opinions expressed are those of the author and do not constitute legal, financial, or business advice. Readers are encouraged to consult with a professional before making any business decisions.

All trademarks, logos, and brand names mentioned in this book are the property of their respective owners. WhatsApp is a registered trademark of Meta Platforms, Inc., and this book is not affiliated with, endorsed by, or sponsored by WhatsApp or Meta.

Again, this book is provided for educational and informational purposes only. While every effort has been made to ensure accuracy, the author and publisher make no guarantees about the results or outcomes from applying the strategies in this book. The success of WhatsApp marketing, Digital marketing, and D2C e-commerce strategies varies based on multiple factors, including industry, execution, customer behaviors, and external conditions.

The author and publisher assume no liability for any losses, business disruptions, or damages that may result from using the information provided in this book. Readers are responsible for conducting their own due diligence and consulting with professional advisors before making business or financial decisions.

The mention of any company, tool, or platform in this book is based on research and experience; however, no official endorsements are implied. WhatsApp is a registered trademark of Meta Platforms, Inc., and again, this book is not affiliated with, endorsed by, or sponsored by WhatsApp or Meta.

By reading this book, you acknowledge that the author and publisher are not responsible for any decisions you make based on its contents.

Disclaimer - The author and publisher are not affiliated with, endorsed by, or promoting any of the brand names, business names, WhatsApp marketing platforms, or CRM tools mentioned in this book. All trademarks, product names, company names, or logos cited herein are the property of their respective owners. References to these names are made purely for informational and illustrative purposes, and do not constitute an endorsement or recommendation.

If you choose to explore or use any of the tools or platforms mentioned, please contact the respective companies directly for the most accurate and up-to-date information.

Why I Wrote This Book

Dear {{First Name}},

I am Aries Ram, and if you're holding this book, chances are you already know WhatsApp isn't just for chatting anymore. But how do you unlock its true marketing power?

That's where most people—my past self included—get stuck.

I wrote "*From Pings to Purchases: WhatsApp Strategies for Digital Marketers*" to change that.

Ten years ago, I was deep in digital marketing, chasing clicks, tweaking landing pages, and watching algorithms rewrite the rules overnight.

I really wish I had known then what I know now: that real revenue lives in real conversations. And WhatsApp is where those conversations are already happening—every day, in real time, with people ready to buy.

This isn't a theory book. It's a playbook. A shortcut. A spark.

It's built from the trenches—drawn from my work with startups, scale-ups, and global brands. And every chapter is designed to give you something practical you can apply immediately, from campaign ideas to automation flows to conversion tactics.

If you're a digital marketer, a founder, or anyone responsible for growth, this book is your map. Not just to more engagement, but to more sales, more retention, and deeper customer relationships.

Because today's best marketing doesn't feel like marketing.

It feels like a conversation between two curious people.

And those who master it?

Win.

So, that's it, let's transform conversations into conversions.

Table of Contents

Introduction: The Channel You've Been Sleeping On

Let me guess – you've run Facebook ads, fine-tuned landing pages, A/B tested subject lines, and maybe even spent late nights inside your CRM, slicing segments and mapping email drips.

You know your funnel.

You know your CAC, *ROAS*, CTR, and *LTV*.

You've optimized the usual suspects – email, social, search, SMS – to the point where gains now come in decimal points, not leaps. You've become an architect of attention in an overcrowded internet. And yet, the ROI needle hasn't moved the way it used to.

Here's the twist: your best-performing marketing channel is probably not one you're paying serious attention to yet.

It's not a platform.

It's not a tactic.

It's not a silver bullet.

It's a **conversation**.

And it's happening right now, inside your customer's WhatsApp inbox.

The New Inbox Economy

Every day, over **3 billion people** open WhatsApp to message friends, family — and increasingly, businesses.

No, not to browse.

Not to scroll.

But to engage.

Directly.

Intimately.

And with an intent.

Yet, most marketers still treat WhatsApp like a spray & pray marketing machine.

But your customers see it as a support tool, not a channel where these see all kinds of offers and discounts blasting in as pings almost every second.

It's still a chat box, not a conversion path.

It's still as a customer service medium, not revenue path.

That's the mistake most marketers make, maybe because of the sales pressure situation they are in.

Now did you know, while you've been spending money on ads to drive traffic to crowded landing pages, some of the smartest brands are driving that same traffic directly into WhatsApp — and **closing sales faster in real time**.

From Funnel to Chat Flow

This book is about shifting your thinking.

From broadcast to dialogue.

From automation to personalization.

From friction to flow.

It's about understanding WhatsApp not just as a messaging app but as a **full-funnel channel** — capable of generating leads, nurturing them, converting them, and keeping them loyal — all from one place.

I'll show you why you must:

- Run Click-to-WhatsApp ad campaigns that outperform your old landing pages
- Build automated welcome flows that hook and qualify leads in under 3 minutes
- Launch broadcast campaigns that feel personal, not pushy
- Use chatbots + human handoffs to close more deals without more headcount
- Recover abandoned carts with a single message
- And build a marketing engine that lives inside your customer's favorite app

Who This Book Is For, Actually!

If you're a **performance driven marketer** who's tired of chasing ever-lower CTRs and ever-higher ad costs...

If you care about **open rates, conversion rates, and lifetime value**, not vanity metrics...

If you're curious about **how to use WhatsApp the right way**, without spamming or burning out your audience...

This book is for you, and it's also a conversation with my younger self who struggled to get orders, repeat purchases, and retain those customers who left without saying anything - even now am clueless as to why they left!

So, Why Now?

Because WhatsApp isn't the future of marketing.

It has already happened — in markets like India, UAE, Spain, Brazil, Indonesia, South Africa, and is rapidly catching fire across Europe and Latin America.

The sooner you learn to speak in "inbox language," the sooner you'll stop begging for attention — and start earning it.

Let's turn that green chat bubble into your most powerful marketing asset.

Let's go from pings... to purchases... soon.

Chapter 1: Your Best Marketing Channel Was in Your Pocket All Along

> *"If you had 98% open rates on your emails, you'd be a legend. On WhatsApp, that's the norm."*

You know the story: Email open rates are declining. Social media reach is throttled unless you pay. Ads are more expensive, more competitive, and less trusted than ever.

We've all read the same reports. We've all felt the same frustration.

We keep optimizing channels that are overused, underperforming, or saturated — and we're fighting to win attention in places where people are just trying to scroll, not shop.

Now, compare that to WhatsApp.

It's personal, real-time, and most importantly, it's welcomed.

It's not just another channel.

It's the inbox that actually gets checked.

The Untapped Superpower of WhatsApp

Let's talk numbers.

- A 98% open rate (source 2024: multiple CRM platforms and WhatsApp marketing providers)
- 45–60% reply rate on well-crafted campaigns
- 3–5x higher conversion rates compared to email or SMS
- Instant visibility – most messages are seen within 5 minutes
- Over 3+ billion users, with the average user checking the app 23–25 times per day

Compare that to email, where you're lucky if 20% open your carefully crafted campaign.
Or Meta ads, where CAC has gone up 70–120% over the last 3 years.

WhatsApp doesn't just beat these channels.

It rewrites the rules of how trust, intent, and conversation convert.

You Don't Need More Channels — You Need More Conversions

Let's be honest: Most of us don't need more traffic.

We need more yield from the traffic we already have.

That's where WhatsApp comes in.

Do you run Meta ads?

Drive them straight into WhatsApp with Click-to-Chat campaigns.

Do you get website visitors?

Offer them a 10% discount via a WhatsApp widget.

Do you send email flows?

Back it up with a message inside the channel they'll actually see.

The final result?

Shorter funnels, faster replies, and warmer leads.

It's not magic — it's just context.

You're catching people where they already spend time, in a format they actually like to use.

The Shift: From Attention-Hunting to Conversation-Starting

We've been trained to chase attention: hook them in the feed, lead them to a funnel, nurture them with content.

That's fine.

But WhatsApp lets you skip the scroll and go straight to the relationship.

It's direct, frictionless, and surprisingly scalable — if you know how to structure your message flows, qualify at the right moments, and automate just enough without sounding robotic.

And no, it's not just for customer support.

It's a full-funnel growth channel: from first touch, to first sale, to repeat business.

Why Digital Marketers Are Late to the WhatsApp Party

Here's the thing: Most digital marketers know of WhatsApp, but they haven't taken it seriously because:

- It wasn't "trackable" like email or ads before.
- It felt "manual" compared to automation tools.
- They didn't realize how much behavior has shifted

But the ecosystem has changed.

Today, you can:

- Run paid campaigns that go directly into chat

- Automate welcome flows and sales qualification

- Broadcast promotional messages (ethically, and with consent)
- Tag, segment, and track user behavior
- Build full-scale funnel automations inside the inbox

Tools like Interakt, WATI, Zoko, and AiSensy have made it easy — even for non-tech marketers to get started in just under 24 hours.

The Opportunity Most Brands Are Missing

Here's a stat to chew on:

A survey by Meta showed that 75% of adults globally want to message with businesses, and over 60% have already done so via WhatsApp or similar platforms.

That means your customers already expect this.

They're waiting.

And chances are, your competitor hasn't figured this out yet — or is still using it as a glorified helpdesk. This is your window.

Action Steps: How to Start Seeing WhatsApp as a Marketing Channel

1. Start tracking inbound conversations as leads, not just support tickets.

2. Test a Click-to-WhatsApp ad — and measure leads and cost versus traditional lead gen.

3. Create a WhatsApp lead magnet (PDF, coupon, mini-course, etc.) and promote it via email or social.

4. Map your existing funnel and identify where a WhatsApp touchpoint would speed up or increase conversion.

5. Study the inbox behavior of your customers: what they respond to, when, and how often.

This isn't just a shiny new tool.

It's a fundamental shift in how customers prefer to engage.

In the next chapter, we'll explore how WhatsApp is more than just a messaging app — it's a mini CRM, a storefront, and a funnel builder all in one screen. Once you see how the pieces connect, you'll never go back to treating it like "just another chat app."

Chapter 2: More Than Messaging — WhatsApp as a Mini-CRM, Storefront, and Funnel

> *"You're thinking of WhatsApp as a messenger. Think of it as a full-funnel marketing platform."*

We've all been conditioned to think in silos.

Marketing generates leads. Sales closes deals. Support answers questions.

And each function uses its own set of tools: CRM, email platform, chatbot, helpdesk, eCommerce platform.

WhatsApp disrupts that.

In a single app — one that your customers already use every day — you can attract, engage, qualify, convert, and retain.

All in one place.

All in real time.

And all in a way that feels personal, not pushy.

If that sounds too good to be true, stick with me — because once you understand how to architect the experience, it starts to look less like a chat app and more like your **leanest, highest-converting growth stack**.

WhatsApp as a Mini-CRM

You don't need Salesforce or HubSpot to keep track of leads. You just need structured conversations and smart tagging.

Inside WhatsApp Business or with third-party tools (like Interakt, Zoko, WATI), you can:

- Tag contacts by interest, behavior, or source (e.g., "Facebook ad – discount code," "Repeat buyer," "High-intent lead")
- Track conversation history — across sales, support, and marketing
- Assign leads to team members with context

- Automate lead scoring based on interaction patterns

- Integrate with your CRM to sync contact data and deal stages

Suddenly, WhatsApp isn't just a messaging app.

It becomes a **dynamic, living customer profile system** — updated in real time based on how people engage with your brand.

And because responses are fast and personal, the data you collect is **richer** and **more actionable** than passive form fills or email clicks.

WhatsApp as a Storefront

Imagine this: A potential customer clicks your ad and opens WhatsApp.

Within seconds, they're greeted with a friendly message:

> "Hey there! Looking for something specific? Let me show you our best-selling styles — or help you grab your 15% discount."

They reply, "Show me designer shirts."

You respond with a **catalog card**, showing images, descriptions, prices, and a "Buy Now" or "Add To Cart" button — all inside the chat.

They tap, add to cart, pay — done.

That's not a future vision.

That's happening **right now** with WhatsApp's built-in commerce features:

- Product catalogs (with images, prices, descriptions)

- Shopping carts
- Payments (in supported countries)
- Deep links to product pages, custom offers, or personalized recommendations
- One click checkouts via third-party integrations (Shopify, WooCommerce, Razorpay, etc.)

The key difference?

There's no website friction.

No tabs to open.

No pages to load.

It's **conversation-led commerce** — and it works.

WhatsApp as a Funnel

Let's go deeper: What if you could run your **entire funnel** – from awareness to sale inside a single WhatsApp thread?

Here's what that could look like:

1. **Lead Capture:** Click-to-WhatsApp ad or website widget brings in a user.

2. **Welcome Flow:** Auto-reply sequence offers options: "Shop Now," "Talk to Support," or "Grab Your Discount."

3. **Segmentation:** User replies "I'm looking for shoes" → tagged as "Footwear – Interested."

4. **Follow-Up:** Automated message 24 hours later: "Hey, still looking for that perfect pair? Here's 10% off."

5. **Conversion:** User purchases directly or chats with a rep to close the deal.

6. **Post-Sale:** Confirmation, upsell/cross-sell options, feedback request.

7. **Retention:** Broadcast message 2 weeks later: "New arrivals just dropped. Want a sneak peek?"

All of this happens **inside WhatsApp**, without switching platforms, dropping cookies, or relying on open rates.

It's tight, targeted, and most of all — it's **customer-controlled**.

Why This Works Better Than Traditional Funnels

- **Fewer steps.** No forms. No redirects.

- **More trust.** It feels like a conversation, not a campaign.

- **More speed.** Responses are instant. Follow-ups are timely.

- **Higher intent.** If someone starts a WhatsApp chat, they're warm.
- **Higher conversions.** Because the human (or human-like) touch still works best.

Most importantly, WhatsApp breaks the pattern of static funnels. It creates **adaptive flows** that respond to what the customer says, not what you assume.

Rethinking Funnel Metrics for WhatsApp

Traditional Funnel:

- Traffic → Landing Page → Form Submit → Email Drip → Sale

WhatsApp Funnel:

- Click → Conversation → Qualification → Offer → Response → Sale

And here's the kicker:

You can measure **every step** using tools that integrate with Meta Ads, CRMs, and chatbot platforms.

Track:

- Cost per WhatsApp lead
- Reply rates
- Time to first response
- Drop-off points in chat
- Conversion rate to sale
- Re-engagement rates

This is **performance marketing, reborn inside a chat**.

Action Steps: Set Up Your WhatsApp Growth Engine

1. Set up a WhatsApp Business API account (or use a partner platform)

2. Create a simple catalog with your top 5–10 products or services

3. Build a welcome flow with 2–3 smart branching options

4. Map the user journey — from first touch to follow-up

5. Tag conversations based on interest, source, or action taken

6. Link your CRM or use native tools to track funnel metrics

7. Run a small campaign and test WhatsApp as your primary funnel

The marketers who win with WhatsApp aren't just "doing chat."

They're reimagining the **customer journey** — one message, one moment, one conversion at a time.

In the next chapter, we'll dive into the secret weapon of WhatsApp growth: the **Click-to-WhatsApp ad**. You'll learn how to run campaigns that skip the landing page entirely — and drop high-intent users straight into the funnel.

Ready to turn clicks into conversations?

Chapter 3: Click-to-WhatsApp Ads: Skipping the Landing Page, Starting the Conversation

> *"Forget landing pages. Send them straight to a real-time conversation."*

In digital marketing, we obsess over conversion rates.

But here's a hard truth: most funnels lose 80–90% of their traffic **before** a visitor even becomes a lead.

Why?

Because we send them to crowded landing pages, force form fills, ask for emails they don't want to give — and by the time they see our offer, they've bounced.

Click-to-WhatsApp ads skip all of that.

Instead of driving traffic to a website, you drive them **straight into a WhatsApp conversation**.

The ad click becomes a chat.

And that chat becomes a qualified lead, a sale, or a loyal customer — all within minutes.

For performance driven marketers, this is a **game-changer**.

Hope you get it now!

What Is a Click-to-WhatsApp Ad?

It's exactly what it sounds like: an ad (usually on Facebook or Instagram) that, when clicked, opens a WhatsApp chat with your business.

But it's more than just a redirect.

- You can **pre-fill the first message**, guiding the user with a call to action like "I want a 15% discount" or "I'm interested in product X."

- You can **personalize the conversation starter** based on the ad creative or audience.

- And you can **automate the reply flow**, qualifying leads or responding instantly, even if your team is offline.

The result is a marketing funnel that feels like a **friendly, instant concierge**, not a cold lead capture system.

Why Click-to-WhatsApp Ads Still Work So Well

1. **Lower Friction**
   No landing page. No form. One click, and they're in the chat.

2. **Higher Intent**
   If someone clicks "Message us on WhatsApp," they're actively looking to engage — not just browsing.

3. **Faster Time to Value**
   You're not waiting hours or days to follow up. You're replying (or automating replies) **immediately**.

4. **Conversation-Led Qualifying**
   Instead of a form with checkboxes, you qualify leads naturally, through conversation: "What's your budget?" or "Which product are you looking for?" or "Do you need help choosing?"

5. **Better Attribution & Retargeting**
   You can track who clicked, who replied, who converted — and retarget based on engagement

level, not just page visits.

Understand with Examples: From Scroll to Sale in Minutes

A fashion D2C brand runs a simple Instagram story ad:

Creative:

Image: A model wearing a new dress.
Text: "Want this look? Get 15% off today."
CTA: "Send Message"

When clicked: WhatsApp opens with a pre-filled message: "Hi, I saw the dress on Instagram. Can I get the 15% offer?"

Sample Auto-reply flow (*set up via WhatsApp API or platform*):

1. "Hey! Great taste. Here's the dress you liked: [image + product link]."

2. “Use code ULOOK15 to grab 15% off. Want help with sizing?”

3. Customer replies, gets answer, and purchases.

Time from click to purchase: **under 7 minutes.**

Zero forms. Zero waiting. Zero drop off.

How to Set Up a Click-to-WhatsApp Ad (Step-by-Step)

1. **Get WhatsApp Business API access**
   You’ll need to use a provider like Interakt, Zoko, or WATI (unless you're a developer managing the API yourself).

2. **Connect your WhatsApp Business number to your Facebook Business Manager**

3. **Go to Meta Ads Manager**

    - Choose the campaign objective: **Messages**

- Choose placement: **Click to Message > WhatsApp**
- Select your connected WhatsApp Business account
- Use ChatGPT build your creative as usual (image, video, headline, CTA)
- Set up the **welcome message** (the pre-filled text users will send)

4. **Create automation flows**
   Use your WhatsApp platform to auto-respond, route leads, or trigger sales flows.

5. **Track and optimize**
   - Measure replies, time to first response, conversion rate
   - A/B test different creatives, CTAs, and welcome messages

  - Retarget users who clicked but didn't reply or didn't convert

Best Practices for High-Converting Click-to-WhatsApp Ads

- **Lead with value** – Don't just say "Message us." Offer something: discount, free consult, early access, quick help.

- **Use urgency and scarcity** – Time-limited offers increase response rates.

- **Pre-qualify with intent** – Example: "Want a free demo?" vs. "Interested in learning more?"

- **Start simple** – Don't overload the user with info in the first message. Prompt one clear reply.

- **Automate smartly** – Use quick replies, buttons, or menus to guide the conversation.

- **Follow up** – If someone drops off mid-chat, follow up within 24 hours with context.

What Not to Do

- Don't treat WhatsApp like email, please. It's not for cold blasts or long-winded newsletters.

- Don't send unsolicited messages without consent, please — it's against WhatsApp's policies and bad for your brand.

- Don't send users into a dead end, please. If someone messages you, have a plan for what happens next: automation, human agent, or next step.

Action Steps: Launch Your First Click-to-WhatsApp Campaign

1. Choose a high-intent offer (discount, product, free consult).

2. Design a simple visual or video that makes the offer clear.

3. Set up your campaign in Meta Ads Manager with WhatsApp as the destination.

4. Craft a welcome message that makes replying easy.

5. Build a 3–5 step follow-up flow to guide users toward purchase or lead qualification.

6. Run a small test with $100–150 and monitor the results.

7. Double down on what works, and scale.

Click-to-WhatsApp ads don't just drive traffic.

They spark conversations, and conversations **close deals faster** than clicks ever could.

In the next chapter, we'll go deep into building **WhatsApp funnels that scale** — automating flows that feel natural, personal, and persuasive.

Now, turn your inbox into a high-performing sales machine.

Let's build your funnel next.

Chapter 4: You've Been Ignoring the Warmest Leads You'll Ever Get

> *"When someone messages your brand, they're not cold — they're ready. But are you?"*

As digital marketers, we've been trained to chase the cold ones.

We obsess over reach. Spend days split-testing creatives. Burn budget on top-of-funnel traffic that *might* click, *might* land, and *might* convert.

And yet, while we're busy optimizing awareness, there's something else happening in the background:

People are messaging your business on WhatsApp right now.

Not to browse.

Not to "stay in touch."

They're reaching out because they're interested.

They're asking questions.

They want answers.

They're giving you a shot.

But are you treating them like the red-hot leads they are?

Or are you ghosting them with a generic reply, leaving them to cool off and disappear?

This chapter is a wake-up call.

Inbound WhatsApp Messages Are Not Just "Support" — They're Sales Waiting to Happen

Most businesses still treat WhatsApp like a helpdesk.

Someone writes in?

Send a templated reply. Maybe get to it in a few hours. Escalate to someone else. End of story.

What they don't realize is: **these are the highest intent leads you'll ever get**.

They came to *you*.

They started the conversation.

They're telling you, without a pixel firing or a form submission: **"I'm interested. Convince me."**

You'd kill for that level of intent from a Google Ad click.

And yet here it is... quietly landing in your WhatsApp inbox, ignored or handled like a ticket.

What Inbound Chat Signals That a Cold Lead Never Will

Let's be clear: when someone messages your brand on WhatsApp, they're not "at the top of the funnel."

They're halfway through it.

They've:

- Seen your product
- Formed an opinion

- Gotten curious enough to act
- Taken the time to reach out on *their* terms

That's not passive behavior — that's **purchase intent**.

This is your window to qualify and convert **within minutes**, not days.

And that's why your WhatsApp strategy shouldn't live in the support department.

It belongs in marketing and sales.

The Psychology of the WhatsApp Buyer

Here's what a typical inbound message tells you:

1. **"I'm not a browser — I'm a buyer with a question."**
   → Treat them like a decision-maker, not a casual visitor.

2. **"I want a response, not a form."**
   → They're choosing the *fastest*, most human way

to talk. So, give them a real conversation.

3. **“I trust WhatsApp more than your site.”**
   → That’s not a knock on your design. It’s just that chats feel personal. Safe. Two-way.

4. **“I expect a fast reply.”**
   → The longer you wait, the colder they get. 15-minute reply time is gold. Under 5? Even better.

How to Build a Sales-Focused Inbound Chat Flow

You don’t need a full-scale sales team replying to every message.

You need a **structured, hybrid flow** — part automation, part human — that knows how to qualify, engage, and convert at scale.

Here's how to build it:

Step 1: Greet Like a Non-bot, Not a Bot

Ditch the boring "Thanks for reaching out, we'll get back to you soon."

Instead, use a smart welcome that:

- **Acknowledges their interest**
- **Hints at value**
- **Opens up next steps**

Example:

"Hey [First Name] You've reached our support team! Are you stuck? Want help choosing the right product or looking for the latest offers?"

Instantly, you've shown presence and opened a lane.

Step 2: Qualify Without the Friction

Don't interrogate. Guide.

Use button replies to segment users:

- "What are you shopping for?"
  → Option A, Option B, Option C

- "Are you looking to buy today or just browsing?"
  → "Ready to buy" / "Need more info"

Tag labels to these contacts or responses in your system so your team knows **who's hot** and who needs nurture.

Step 3: Deliver Value Fast

Based on the answers, send:

- Product links
- Explainer videos
- Limited-time offers

- Comparison charts
- Testimonials

Make sure these feel personalized, not generic.

This is where automation helps — but human review (or smart logic) makes it work.

Step 4: Route to the Right Team (or Closer)

High-ticket product? Service business? Route the chat to sales.

Shopping query with a pricing question? Route to commerce or support. This is also called topic-based agent routing.

Use **chat routing rules** based on tags, keywords, or workflow paths — most modern WhatsApp chatbot or commerce platforms offer this.

And if you're not using routing? You're wasting qualified leads on the wrong people.

Step 5: Follow Up Like a Human, at Scale

If someone stops replying, don't disappear.

Instead, drop a timed message (within WhatsApp's 24-hour reply window):

- "You still need help choosing the right option?"
- "BTW, the offer you saw earlier expires in the next 2 hours."
- "Here's what others loved from our collection."

Even better, ask a question to invite re-engagement.

How to Scale Without Losing the Personal Touch

This is where most marketers mess up.

They either go all manual (and drop the ball), or all automation (and lose the human tone).

The key is **hybrid scale**:

- Let automation handle routing, FAQs, and top level flows.

- Let real humans step in at the right moment — especially when there's high purchase intent.

Think of it like a relay race.

Bots run the first lap and handover the baton to...

And Humans take the baton for the final sprint.

Use platforms like: WATI, Zoko, Interakt or AiSensy.

If You Take One Thing from This Chapter...

Then it's this - every inbound WhatsApp message is a signal.

A flare in the night. A hand raised. A wallet half-open.

Ignore it, and you're burning cash.

Respond with care, speed, and structure — and you'll unlock the kind of ROI that cold ads only dream of.

So, the next time your WhatsApp buzzes with a new message, don't think just "support."

Think: **This is a warm lead. This is your moment.**

Let's close.

Chapter 5: Welcome Flows that Hook, Qualify, and Convert in Under 3 Minutes

> *"That first 'Hey ' message is your golden moment. Don't waste it."*

Here's something most marketers miss:

The most valuable part of a WhatsApp conversation is the first 180 seconds.

If you don't capture attention, set context, and guide the user forward in those first few exchanges, you've lost them — even if they don't leave right away.

And yet, most brands start with something like:

> "Hey, Thank you for contacting us. We will get back to you shortly."

That's not a welcome. That's a door half closed.

Let's be clear:

Your welcome flow is your hook, your funnel, and **your first conversion opportunity — all rolled into one.**

If you get it right, the rest of the funnel builds itself.

If you get it wrong, everything downstream struggles.

So, let's talk about what a high-performing WhatsApp welcome flow *actually* looks like — and how to build one that qualifies and converts without sounding like a bot.

First Things First: Why the Welcome Flow Matters

That initial WhatsApp message?

It's not just your first impression — it's your **only** shot at attention.

Because people don't scroll on WhatsApp. They don't browse.

They don't "check later."

They either reply *now*... or they ghost you.

So your welcome message has one job: **Spark action.**

It should get the user to do something *useful* — tap a button, reply with an option, or click a link — within the first 2–3 messages.

If it doesn't?

You're bleeding leads you already paid for.

The Golden Rules of a Great Welcome Flow

1. **Sound like a human, not a ticket system.**
   Drop the "Dear customer" tone. Speak like you would in a real-life conversation — friendly, brief, direct.

2. **Give immediate value or context.**
   Don't make them wait. Either acknowledge their intent ("Here's that discount you clicked for!") or offer help instantly ("Let's find what you're looking for.")

3. **Use buttons or quick replies — don't ask open-ended questions too early.**
   Make it easy for people to respond with a tap, not a paragraph. It increases engagement and helps you guide the journey.

4. **Segment silently.**
   Every tap or reply is a data point. Use it to tag, segment, and qualify users without making them feel like they're filling a form.

Anatomy of a High-Converting Welcome Flow

Here's a simple, swipeable structure you can customize for almost any business:

Message 1 – Greet + Set Context

> "Hey You made it! Ready to explore our best offers or need help picking the right product?"

Message 2 – Present Clear CTA Options

- Shop New Arrivals
- Claim Your 10% Discount
- Talk to a Human

Message 3 – Auto-responder Based on Selection

If they tap "***Claim Discount***":

> “Great choice. Here’s your exclusive 10% code: *SAVE10*. Tap below to start shopping”
> [***Shop Now Button***]

If they tap "***Talk to a Human***":

> “Hang tight — we’re connecting you with a team member now. While you wait, want to see what’s trending today?”

Each branch becomes a mini-funnel based on user intent.

They came for the deal?

Give it, then nudge toward product suggestions.

They need support?

Route them fast, but keep them engaged with helpful links while they wait.

They’re exploring?

Start a guided quiz or product finder.

The secret: **every path leads toward conversion or qualification.**

Please, *Please* Avoid These Common Mistakes

- **Overloading the first message with info.**
  Don't throw your entire brand story at them in one breath. You're not pitching — you're starting a conversation.

- **Forgetting to track responses.**
  Every button click should tag the user (e.g., "Interested in Shoes", "Clicked Discount"), so your follow-ups are personalized.

- **Sounding too robotic.**
  "Please select from the following options to proceed" feels cold.
  "Let's get you to the good stuff — what are you looking for today?" feels warm.

- **Creating dead ends.**
  Every button and response should lead to the next step — don't drop users in limbo with no clear action.

Flow Templates by Intent

For eCommerce / Retail:

> "Hey! You caught us just in time — our weekend offer's live. Want to see deals, shop new drops, or ask a question?"

Options:

- ❖ Show Me Deals
- ❖ What's New
- ❖ Need Help

For Service Businesses / Consultants:

> "Hi! Ready to book a call, download our pricing guide, or see success stories?"

Options:

- Book a Call
- View Pricing
- Case Studies

For Lead Magnets / Funnels:

> "Welcome! Want your free guide, or prefer to chat with someone about your needs?"

Options:

- Get the Guide
- Talk to Sales

Add Personalization Without the Creep Factor

- Use the user's **first name** if you've captured it in the ad or previous message.
- Mention **the source of the chat** ("You clicked our IG ad for skin care tips").
- Reference their last action, if applicable ("You were checking out our project pricing page").

Keep it relevant, not invasive.

Automation Tools That Nail the Welcome Game

These tools make it easy to build logic-based welcome flows:

- **WATI** – Tag users based on replies, segment automatically
- **Zoko** – Product recommendation flows with buttons + discounts
- **Interakt** – Great for onboarding and abandoned cart tie-ins

Whichever tool you use, make sure it supports:

- Button/quick reply logic
- Tag-based segmentation
- Message sequencing
- Human agent handoff

Your 3-Minute Mission: Hook. Qualify. Convert.

The first reply is where trust is built.

The second reply is where intent is revealed.

The third reply is where direction is set.

Don't waste those three messages on filler.

Use them to lead your audience forward — with clarity, speed, and value.

If your welcome flow feels like a warm, helpful guide rather than a faceless bot...

Yeah, good job, you're doing it right!

Chapter 6: Broadcasts That Don't Feel Like Blasts

> *"If your WhatsApp campaign feels like a mass message, you've already lost."*

Broadcasting on WhatsApp is a high-stakes game.

Done right, it's a conversion machine.

Done wrong, it's an unsubscribe trigger. And naturally Meta blocks your number.

And the difference?

Tone, timing, targeting — and the illusion of intimacy.

Because unlike email, WhatsApp is personal by default.

It's where people talk to their mom, their best friend, their date, their landlord, their boss, their client – right?

If your message crashes into that space like a generic, pushy brand alert.

You're not just ignored.

You're ***blocked***.

So, here's the hard truth:

If your WhatsApp broadcast *feels* like a bulk message... it fails before it even lands.

This chapter is your playbook for avoiding that fate — and building WhatsApp campaigns that convert *because* they feel like 1:1 conversations, not 1-to-thousands broadcasts.

Why WhatsApp Broadcasting Isn't Email Marketing 2.0

Let's get this out of the way:

- **There's no subject line.** You've got to hook from the first words of the message itself.
- **There's no inbox preview.** You show up as a notification. You either get read — or swiped away.
- **There's no tolerance for spam.** You need opt-in. And you need relevance.

WhatsApp marketing is not about shouting louder.

It's about whispering smarter.

The Broadcast Equation That Works

Every winning broadcast is built on three core pillars:

1. **Segmentation** – Don't message everyone. Message the right people.

2. **Personalization** – Don't send the same message. Send the *right version.*

3. **Intent Timing** – Don't send it *when it's ready.* Send it when *they're ready.*

Let’s break that down.

1. Segment Like You Actually Know Them

This is where most brands get lazy.

They import one big contact list and hit "send."

But WhatsApp is not your newsletter.

It’s your **most intimate marketing channel**.

So, treat it like a conversation, not a blast.

Segment based on:

- **What they clicked or opted in for** (e.g., “Joined via skincare quiz ad”)
- **What they bought** (e.g., “First-time customer” vs “Repeat buyer”)
- **How recently they engaged** (e.g., “Last active 2 days ago”)
- **What they asked for** (e.g., “Requested pricing” or “Demo follow-up”)

Even basic segmentation like “Men’s vs Women’s collection” or “Product interest: shoes vs bags” can dramatically boost engagement.

Pro tip:

Use tagging inside your welcome flows and post-purchase chats to silently segment users *before* your next broadcast ever goes out.

2. Hyper Personalization That Feels Natural — Not Creepy

Adding someone’s name isn’t enough.

The message has to feel like it was *written for them* — not just *addressed to them.*

Let’s compare:

❌ “Hey You, check out our new arrivals!”

✅ “Hey Sam — we just dropped 5 new summer styles in your size - Want a sneak peek?”

See the difference?

The second one feels like a message from someone who *knows what you care about.*

Hyper Personalization tactics that actually move the needle:

- Reference what they viewed: "You asked about our skincare bundles..."
- Mention timing: "It's been a week since your last order — need a refill?"
- Tie it to context: "We noticed you saved your cart but didn't check out..."

And don't overdo it.

WhatsApp is casual.

Friendly.

Natural.

You don't need to mimic a chatbot with {{*FirstName*}} and {{*ProductInterest*}} every other line. Just... sounds real.

3. Send It When They're Most Likely to Care

Timing isn't just about "what time of day."

It's about *where they are in the buyer journey.*

A few examples:

- **Post-click retargeting:** Someone clicked a "Free Trial" ad but didn't complete signup?

  Hit them 15 minutes later:

  "Need help setting up your free trial? Just reply and we'll walk you through it."

- **Abandoned cart flow:** Send 2 hours later, not 24.

  "Hey, saw you left this behind - Still want it? Your 12% discount is still active for the next hour."

- **New drop for loyal buyers:** Target people who bought similar products in the last 30 days.

> "New drop alert 👟 You're gonna love this one. Early access just for you."

And yes — **time of day still matters.**

Avoid early mornings or late nights.

Send between **10 AM** and **7 PM local time** for best engagement, unless you know their time zone behavior.

The Broadcast Blueprint (Swipe This)

Here's a basic flow for a broadcast that doesn't feel like one:

Step 1: Hook
First line = reason to care.

> "Guess what just dropped in your size"

Step 2: Personal Touch
Mention what they liked, viewed, or bought.

> "You grabbed the beige tote last month — this one's its bold sister."

Step 3: CTA + Value
Make it action-oriented, and give them a reason.

> "Tap below for early access. First 100 get free shipping."

Step 4: Optional Follow-Up (1–2 Hours Later)
If they didn't click:

> "Hey — just checking, did you want to see the drop? It's moving fast."

This feels like a friend nudging them toward something cool — not a brand pushing an offer.

Some Tools That Can Make This Work

- **Interakt** – Segment-based broadcasts with opt-in flows
- **WATI** – Rich broadcast analytics and personalization
- **Zoko/AiSensy** – Ecommerce specific flows + cart behavior triggers

Make sure your tool supports:

- Tag-based segmentation
- Message personalization
- Message templates (for approval)
- Delivery reports + click tracking

What Success Looks Like From My POV

Here's what we're seeing with well-run WhatsApp broadcasts:

- **Open rates:** 90%+
- **Reply rates:** 25–35%
- **Click-throughs:** 15–20%
- **Conversions:** 5–12%, depending on offer + flow

Compare that to email (2–5% click rate, if you're lucky), and the case builds itself.

Broadcasts That Feel Like Conversations - Win Every Time

The real magic of WhatsApp?

It's the only channel where marketing can *feel like messaging*.

The moment it starts feeling like a "campaign," you've lost.

But if it feels like something *meant for me...*

I'll click. I'll reply. I'll buy.

So, the next time you hit "Send Broadcast," ask yourself:

Would *you* open this message if it landed in your phone right now?

If the answer isn't yes, rewrite it until it is.

Chapter 7: WhatsApp Funnels Are the New Email Funnels

"Inbox marketing is shifting. You're still designing flows for the wrong inbox."

If you're still building elaborate email nurture sequences even today, like it's 2015, I've got news for you:

Your best customers have moved on in life a bit.

They're not living in Gmail anymore.

They're not scrolling through newsletters.

They're replying to voice notes while waiting in line.

They're tapping through product links between meetings.

They're searching about topics on AI platforms, almost saying bye *bye* to Google.

And they're on **WhatsApp.**

But you?

Are you still trying to warm them up with 6-part email drips they might never even open or see.

This chapter is your wake up call – I hope!

We're going to reframe some **funnels** for the platform your users *actually* respond to — where engagement rates haven't flatlined, and where behavior looks nothing like what traditional marketers were trained for.

The Myth of the Modern Email Funnel

Let's be honest:

Email nurture used to work.

Step 1: Opt-in.

Step 2: Value-driven content over 5–7 emails.

Step 3: CTA to book, buy, or try.

That model is dying.

Why?

- **Open rates have plummeted** (hello, Gmail tabs and iOS privacy).

- **Mobile behavior dominates** — people don't "read," they tap.

- **Decision cycles are shorter** — your audience needs fewer emails, more direction.

You don't need *more emails.*

You need **smarter conversations** — the kind that happen naturally on WhatsApp.

WhatsApp Isn't Just a Channel. It's a Funnel.

Let's flip the mental model:

Instead of **"sending a sequence,"** You're now **building a journey that reacts in real-time.**

Every tap, reply, or silence becomes a signal.

And you build your funnel around that signal, not a fixed schedule.

Here's the core idea:

Behavioral sequences > Time Based sequences.

Email says: “Send email #3 on Day 4.”

WhatsApp says: “They tapped ‘Not sure yet’ — trigger a message asking what’s holding them back.”

Big difference.

Anatomy of a WhatsApp Funnel

Let’s break down the essential stages of a WhatsApp-based nurture funnel:

1. The Entry Point

Your user opts in via:

- Ads that click-to-WhatsApp
- Website popup / lead magnet
- Checkout form
- QR code in-store or on packaging

Key rule: Make the entry message *contextual.*

> "You downloaded our skin care guide —
> ready to build your custom routine?"

You're not starting cold. They've already raised their hand.

2. The Micro-Qualifier

Instead of bombarding them with info, ask one useful question:

> "Quick question — what's your #1 skin concern right now?"

Give options via buttons:

- Acne
- Dryness
- Aging
- Uneven tone

Now you've got a signal — and a segment.

3. The Personalized Value Drop

This is your "email value content," but compressed, visual, and casual.

> "Got it! Here's a quick 30-sec read on tackling acne the right way. Plus, a product we swear by: *ClearSkin Serum*. Want to check it out?"

Send:

- A carousel
- A 15-sec product demo
- A link to see reviews

Let them explore.

Keep it low-pressure.

4. The Engagement Split

If they tap or reply:

> "Want help choosing the right bundle? I can guide you ✋"

Now they're in a **purchase-intent flow.**

If they ghost:

Wait 24 hours.

Then:

> "Still thinking? We just added a free consultation if you'd like help deciding."

You're reactivating intent without being pushy.

5. The Purchase Path

Once they're engaged:

- Show limited-time bundles
- Add urgency
- Offer chat support

> "This bundle is 20% off till midnight. Want me to hold one for you?"

Use buttons:

- Yes, reserve it
- Not yet
- Have a question

Every reply = more signal = more flow logic.

6. The Post Purchase Follow Up Reality

Here's where most brands drop the ball.

After someone buys, *don't go silent.*

WhatsApp is your moment to shine:

- Confirm purchase (not just with order ID — with excitement)
- Send care tips
- Offer a referral
- Ask for a review (with tap-to-reply)

> "Your order is on the way, while you wait, here's how to get the most out of your serum. PS: Want 10% off your next one for referring a friend?"

That's retention, referrals, and LTV — all baked in.

WhatsApp Funnel vs Email Funnel: A *Side-by-Side* Look

📩 **Email Funnel**	💬 **WhatsApp Funnel**
Time-based sends	Behavior-based triggers
Text-heavy	Tap-to-skim, visual-first
Often ignored	High open + reply rate
Feels like marketing	Feels like messaging
Hard to personalize at scale	Easy to personalize with tags + buttons

The Power of Post-Click Retargeting

Let's say a user clicked your WhatsApp ad but didn't convert.

Instead of dropping them into a 5-day email sequence...

Send a contextual WhatsApp message **15 minutes later.**

> "You clicked our free trial but didn't finish setting it up — want help?"

Or if they started filling a quiz and stopped:

> "Still interested in your personalized workout plan? Tap below to pick up where you left off."

This is where WhatsApp crushes every other channel — *immediacy + context + high open rate.*

Tips That Make It Work

You'll need a platform that supports:

- Triggered flows
- Tags and segments
- Button-based replies
- Conditional logic

Some great picks that I have used:

- **Typebot** – Visual funnel builder inside WhatsApp
- **WATI** – Behavioral flows + segmentation
- **Zoko** – Ecom-specific logic, great for retargeting
- **Landbot** – For quiz-style funnels
- **Respond.io** – Robust workflows + CRM sync

Start Small. Scale Smart.

Don't try to replicate your 15-email sequence on WhatsApp.

That's not the point.

Start with:

1. A strong welcome flow
2. One behavioral path to product
3. A post-purchase loop

Then test, tag, and optimize.

Your new funnel isn't a campaign.

It's a conversation — one that learns, adapts, and sells.

Chapter 8: You're Not Automating Enough — or in the Right Places

"Automation isn't just about speed. It's about not missing the moment."

Now let's cut to it:

You're *probably* using automation the wrong way.

Or worse — barely using it at all.

Most digital marketers hear "automation" and immediately think of chatbots that sound like robots or FAQ menus that no one actually reads.

But here's the thing:

WhatsApp isn't just a chat app.

It's a timing-sensitive, behavior-reactive, conversion engine.

If you're not automating *strategically*, you're leaving money on the table. Daily.

This chapter is about shifting how you think about automation.

Not as a way to "save time."

But as a way to **never miss the moment when your customer is ready.**

Because when someone's buying signals show up on WhatsApp — you **have seconds, not hours, to respond.**

Let's fix that.

Automation Isn't Just for "Support"

Most brands only use automation for two things:

1. Auto-replies like: "Thanks for messaging! We'll get back to you soon."

2. A janky FAQ menu that looks like it was built in 2017.

That's not automation.

That's *deflection*.

Real WhatsApp automation is proactive. Reactive. Contextual.

It's built to guide people, not just "hold them" until a human shows up.

And more importantly — **it's invisible when done right.**

Here's Where You *Should* Be Automating

Let's walk through the high-leverage points. These are moments where automation can quietly — but powerfully — drive sales, support, and loyalty.

1. Instant FAQs That Actually Solve the Problem

Don't send people to a help center.

Don't make them wait.

Design your FAQ flow to *answer and qualify at the same time.*

Example:

> "Need help with something?"

- ❖ Order Status
- ❖ Refund or Exchange
- ❖ Shipping Info
- ❖ Product Help

If they tap "*Order Status*":

> "Got it — just reply with your order ID, or tap to fetch with your phone number."

Bonus: Route high-friction issues to a human right away.

Don't trap them in a loop.

2. Cart Recovery That Feels Like a Friend Reminding You

A user adds to the cart, then vanishes.

Do you:

❌ Email them 12 hours later with a boring reminder?

✅ Or WhatsApp them in 15 minutes with something like:

> "Hey — you left the Mango Orange Bliss Scented Candle in your cart - Want me to reserve it for you? It's selling fast."

Add buttons:

- Yes, complete order
- Not now
- Got questions

The magic isn't just in speed. It's in **relevance + timing.**

No brand voice, no pressure — just a nudge that *feels human.*

3. Back-in-Stock Alerts That Beat Your Competitors

When an item's out of stock, make it easy to opt in:

> "This one's a bestseller! Want us to WhatsApp you when it's back?"

Then — automate the return message the *minute* it's available again:

> "It's back Mango Orange Bliss Candle just restocked. Want me to add one to your cart?"

One tap = frictionless buying.

And because it's on WhatsApp?

It actually gets read.

4. Event-Based Messages That Drive Behavior

Think birthday discounts, trial expirations, limited-time drops — but smarter.

Instead of “Happy Birthday! Here’s 10% off.”
send:

> “Happy Birthday, Nina, We built you a custom bundle — ready to unwrap it?”

Button: [*Show Me My Gift*]

Or if a trial is ending:

> “2 days left in your trial. Want to unlock bonus features before it ends?”

This is the future of CRM: automated, 1-to-1 messages that look like *you thought of them*, right on time.

5. Loyalty Flows That Don't Feel Like Loyalty Flows

Want retention?

Use automation to:

- Congratulate users when they hit a milestone
- Remind them of unused points
- Offer early access to drops
- Ask for feedback *at the right time*

Example:

> "You've placed 3 orders with us in 2 months. That officially makes you a VIP. Hence, can we give you an early access to next week's drop?"

Feels like recognition.

Not marketing.

"But What If They Want to Talk to a Human?"

Good.

Let them! (*just like how "Mel Robbins" says*).

But do it *smartly*.

Here's the best chatbot-to-human handoff structure:

1. Bot handles the simple stuff: order lookups, product suggestions, and qualifying questions.

2. If the user types anything outside of those flows or taps "Talk to a human," trigger a seamless transfer.

3. Send:
   "One sec — connecting you to a real human Sit tight."

Route to support, sales, or your closer team.

Pro tip: Don't just hand off. **Give the human full context.**

Tags, chat history, and last action — all visible in the agent dashboard.

The conversation should feel continuous, not like starting over.

Don't Try to Automate Everything — Just the *Moments That Matter*

This isn't about replacing people.

It's about scaling attention.

So don't build a chatbot that tries to replace your sales team.

Build flows that *spot* opportunity and hand off *at the right time.*

Use automation to:

- Answer fast
- Respond contextually
- Act instantly when a signal pops

Your competition is still stuck in live chat queues and delayed follow-ups.

You?

You've built a system that *responds faster than they can Google your competitor.*

Some Tools That Help You Nail This

- **WATI** – Smart flows, great for cart + event triggers
- **Zoko/AiSensy** – Ecommerce friendly, deep Shopify integrations
- **Interakt** – Clean bot-to-human handoff setup
- **Typebot** – Great for visual flows, quizzes, lead capture
- **Respond.io** – For complex routing and CRM logic

Look for tools that support:

- Button-based flows
- Trigger conditions
- Variables and tagging
- Human-agent escalation

It's Not About the Bot; It's About that Moment.

Automation doesn't win because it's "faster."

It wins because it shows up **right when it matters.**

When a cart is abandoned.

When a product restocks.

When someone's on the fence and a helpful nudge would tip them over.

That's the game.

Not blasting messages. Not showing off your tech stack.

Just showing up — *on time, in context, like a human would.*

Chapter 9: Conversations Close Sales (And Recover Abandoned Carts Too)

> *"That cart might be abandoned. But it's still sitting in their inbox."*

Let's get real for a second:

Abandoned carts aren't lost.

They're just *unfinished conversations*.

That "almost-customer"? They're not gone.

They just needed a little more time, context, or confidence.

And if you're still relying on a dusty email reminder to bring them back, I've got news:

You're playing the wrong game.

Because on **WhatsApp**, that abandoned cart isn't just a statistic.

It's still sitting there — *inside a chat thread* they opened.

A live, tappable, messageable space you can re-enter at any moment.

That's not a drip campaign.

That's a door.

Still slightly open.

And in this chapter, we're going to talk about how to walk through it — and close.

Cart Recovery: Rethink the Timing, Tone, and Trigger

Most digital marketers treat abandoned cart recovery like this:

- Wait 1–6 hours.
- Send a cold email with a generic subject line.
- Maybe include a coupon.
- Hope for a click.

You've seen the results — *meh.*

But on **WhatsApp**?

You can re-engage while the intent is still warm.

Try this:

> **15–30 minutes** after abandonment:
> "Hey! Looks like you left these behind,
> Want us to hold them for you, [*First Name*]
> before they sell out?"

Add quick-reply buttons:

- Complete My Order
- Not Now
- I've Got a Question

It feels human, at least.

It's fast.

It puts the user back in control — and it works.

The Key Ingredient: Personalization at Scale

The power of WhatsApp isn't just timing.

It's *context.*

When someone gets a message like:

> "Still thinking about the Espresso Starter Kit? It's in someone else's cart too, Want us to save one for you?"

...it doesn't feel like marketing.

It feels like *help*.

Here's how to personalize without writing 50 different messages:

- Use product names dynamically (from cart or quiz data)
- Mention their last action: "You were almost done with checkout..."
- Reference scarcity or reviews: "9 left in stock. 123 5-star ratings."
- Show empathy: "Not sure which flavor's right? I can help you choose."

It's not creepy.

Its conversational commerce done – right?

Manual + Automated = The Recovery Power Combo

Let's be clear: You don't need a live agent replying to every cart.

But there's a sweet spot.

Automated first touch + human backup = scalable AND personal.

Example Flow:

1. **Automation**: 20 minutes post-abandonment

   "Forgot something? Your order's still waiting."

2. User taps **"Need Help"**
   → **Live agent** jumps in:

   "Hey! Happy to help. Was there something holding you back?"

   Now, that's how you move a hesitant buyer into a confident one.

Cold Leads Aren't Dead — They're Dormant

Now let's talk about leads that didn't even get to cart.

Maybe they clicked your ad. Started a quiz. Messaged your bot. Then ghosted.

Good news: **They're still reachable.**

The chat is *still there* on their phone. And when you message them again — it's not out of the blue. It's just picking up where they left off.

Try:

> "Still want your free haircare routine? I saved your results — just tap below to finish the quiz."

or

> "Saw you checked out our coaching plan last week. Got a new case study that might interest you "

If you're using tools like WATI, Interakt, AiSensy or Zoko, you can tag these leads and trigger reactivation flows after 3, 7, or 14 days of inactivity.

Don't Just Recover — Upsell While You're There

Here's the secret sauce: **Every recovered cart is a chance to increase AOV.**

After a user completes a recovered purchase, trigger this:

> "Your order's confirmed!
> Want to add the cleaning kit for just $7 more? It ships free with your bundle."

OR

> "Quick heads up — customers who bought this also grabbed these"

Now you're not just recovering lost sales — You're expanding them.

Think of it like conversational cross-sell.

One tap, one thoughtful nudge, one upgraded order.

The Psychology of Re-Engagement I have Tried: Use Scarcity, Curiosity, and Reciprocity

Great WhatsApp recovery messages use *emotional levers* — but subtly.

Here's how:

- **Scarcity**: "Only 5 left in stock — want me to hold one for you?"

- **Curiosity**: "We just added a surprise gift to your cart — Ready to check it out?"

- **Reciprocity**: "We saved your cart AND added a 10% thank-you — valid for the next hour."

You're not manipulating.

You're guiding.

And when done right, it doesn't feel like a funnel — it feels like help.

Pro Tip: Don't Just Wait — Create Reasons to Come Back

Want to re-engage without sounding like a "reminder"?

Use these triggers:

- Price drops
- New variants or styles
- Restocks
- Limited bundles
- Free shipping windows
- Bonus gifts for fast action
- Cash on delivery option

Example:

> "Your coffee press is back — and this week, it comes with a free bean sampler. Want me to reserve one?"

Now your message isn't annoying. It's *anticipated.*

Quick Recovery Templates to Swipe & Use

Cart Recovery

> "You left these in your cart – Still want them?"
>
> [✅ Yes, finish my order]
>
> [❌ Not right now]
>
> [⁉️ Got a question]

Reactivation

"Still curious about the productivity course? I've got a new module sneak peek if you want it."

[🎥 Show Me]

[📅 Book a Demo]

[❌ Not Interested]

Upsell Post-Purchase

"Thanks for your order! Want to add the travel pouch for just $5 more before we ship?"

[✅ Yes, Add It]

[❌ I'm Good]

Treat Every Conversation Like a Second Chance

In WhatsApp marketing, the funnel *never really ends.*

It loops.

It pauses.

It resumes.

A cart, a click, a ghosted message — they're not dead ends.

They're invitations to re-engage with empathy, timing, and value.

The brands that win?

They don't chase customers.

They continue the conversation — one thoughtful message at a time.

Chapter 10: The Smart Marketer's WhatsApp Stack & KPI Playbook

> *"You track open rates. But do you track reply rates, read windows, and response quality?"*

Let's be honest:

If you're running WhatsApp like it's just another broadcast channel, you're missing the point — and the profit.

You're not in the business of *sending messages.*

You're in the business of *starting conversations that convert.*

And just like you wouldn't run an email campaign without tracking open rates, clicks, A/B test results, and ROI — WhatsApp demands its own metrics, tools, and mindset.

This chapter is your **smart marketer's playbook** for building the right stack, tracking the right KPIs, and optimizing the one inbox that actually talks back.

First, the Stack: What You Need (and What You Don't)

You don't need a 27-tool Frankenstack.

But you *do* need the right setup for reach, automation, insights, and handoffs.

Here's a no-fluff stack to run a high-performance WhatsApp operation:

1. WhatsApp API Provider

This is your foundation. Choose one that has or helps you:

- Get a verified blue tick or support in getting it.
- Contact management and tagging.
- Broadcasts with auto-segmentation.
- eCommerce Store Builder, Chatbot Automation + live agent handoff.

- Mini CRM/ Shopify or WooCommerce integrations.

My Top Picks:

- **WATI** – Best for ecommerce and D2C brands.
- **Zoko/AiSensy** – Excellent for Shopify users.
- **Gupshup** – Scalable and API-rich.
- **Interakt** – Clean UI, good automation.

Pro Tip: Choose one that lets you see *conversation-level analytics,* not just delivery stats.

2. Automation Builder

This is your flow engine — for welcome sequences, quizzes, recovery flows, etc.

Must-haves:

- Drag-and-drop UI
- Conditional logic
- Dynamic content (e.g., cart items, names, quiz results)
- Bot-to-human fallback
- Event triggers from your site/app

3. CRM or Ecommerce Integration

If you can't *see* the user journey — you can't personalize it.

Make sure you connect:

- Shopify / WooCommerce / Magento
- HubSpot / Zoho / Salesforce
- Or your custom backend via webhooks or APIs

This is what lets you say:

> "Still thinking about the Red Sneakers in size 10?"
> Instead of - "Hi! We noticed you left something in your cart."

Then, the FOMO Metrics: What Actually Matters

You're not just trying to "increase reach."

You're trying to *start and steer meaningful conversations.*

So don't just track **send** and **seen**.

Track what actually reflects intent and action.

Here's your new WhatsApp KPI dashboard, that I have in mind for success:

1. Reply Rate

Forget open rates.

WhatsApp is *read by default.*

Instead, ask:

- How many recipients *replied* to your broadcast?
- What % of leads engage with your first message?

> Benchmark to beat: **15–30%** reply rate for well targeted campaigns.

2. Read Window Timing

You have **24 hours** to message a user after they reply.

So track:

- When they read
- How fast they respond
- How long it takes your team to reply

Speed = conversions.

3. Response Quality

Don't just count replies.

Analyze them:

- Are users asking questions? (High intent)
- Are they confused? (Fix messaging)
- Are they ghosting after the bot? (Improve flows)

Tag conversations. Review transcripts. Optimize fast.

4. Click-to-Conversion Rates

If you're linking to pages (product, cart, booking), track:

- Click-throughs from WhatsApp
- Add-to-cart and purchase rates
- Conversion lag (how long from first message to sale)

Use UTM tags + your ecommerce analytics.

5. Conversation Value

How much revenue does a WhatsApp conversation generate?

Track:

- Revenue from recovered carts
- Average order value uplift via upsells
- Bookings or lead conversions traced back to chat

Assign value per conversation — like you do with CPL (Cost Per Lead) or CAC (Customer Acquisition Cost).

> **Hint**: Tools like Zoko and WATI can attribute revenue per WhatsApp conversation, not just per ad or session.

Message Testing: How to *Actually* A/B Test in WhatsApp

Yes, you *can* test subject lines, CTA buttons, and copy — even in WhatsApp.

Here's how:

1. **Create two broadcast versions**

    - Change only *one* variable: Headline, Offer, CTA, Image

2. **Send to a test segment** (500–1,000 users max)

3. **Track:**
    - Reply rate
    - Click rate
    - Positive response sentiment (manual or tagged)
4. **Scale the winner**

Bonus: WhatsApp has no algorithm filtering. If your test flops, it flops honestly. Use that feedback.

Measuring ROI: It's More Than Just Clicks

Here's what separates amateurs from smart marketers:

You don't just measure ROI by clicks.

You measure it by *conversations that convert.*

Your WhatsApp ROI formula might look like:

```
(Total Revenue from WhatsApp Leads -
Monthly WhatsApp Costs) ÷

Monthly WhatsApp Costs
```

Or more granular:

- Recovery Rate per 100 carts
- Cost per Conversation (if using ads to WhatsApp)
- Revenue per Broadcast
- CLTV of users acquired via WhatsApp vs other channels

Make WhatsApp its *own line item* in your performance report.

Your Mastery Lives in the Metrics

You're not just sending messages anymore.

You're engineering micro-moments that move people.

And just like you obsess over email flows or ad CTRs, WhatsApp deserves its own dashboard, its own rhythm, its own growth engine.

Because here's the truth:

The brands that scale through WhatsApp don't do it by accident.

They test, track, and tweak until the inbox becomes a revenue stream.

Now you've got the playbook.

It's time to build the stack.

Watch the right signals.

And run WhatsApp like the performance channel it's becoming.

So, Why WhatsApp Is the Future of D2C Retention Marketing

"The brands that win tomorrow aren't louder — they're closer."

WhatsApp isn't just a messaging app, and you know it by now, at least after reading all those 10 chapters, else, make a U-turn now before FOMO starts.

It has become the most intimate, most opened, most action ready inbox your customer has.

In a world where AI is supporting every Marketer to power up their daily tasks at work, your emails get filtered, ads get skipped, and cookies are going extinct — **conversation is your new conversion channel**; just blindly trust my 15+ years of exposure in Marketing and Sales across B2C, B2B and D2C industries when I say this!

And retention?

Forget it if you're not opening ears, eyes, and even your nose to your customers.

That's not built with email blasts.

It's built with presence, timing, and relevance.

If you're specifically in D2C, the gold is no longer in how many you reach — it's in ***who replies***.

Right or *Wrong*?

Because retention isn't about getting a second sale.

It's about making your customer feel like they never left your store and that now it has become a habit to buy your products wherever they are!

And, Why Should You, as a Digital Marketer, Learn WhatsApp Marketing?

I don't know, you tell me why?

Because you read my book and you somehow figured out that - this isn't "just another channel."

It's a new muscle. It's like salt in your dish. It's like sugar in your coffee, or It's like masala in your Biriyani...

Learning WhatsApp is learning:

- How to not just sell, but sell with empathy via conversations.

- How to not just automate, but automate without losing your human edge.

- How to not just ask customers to be loyal, but turn conversations into loyalty loops.

- How to not just build a brand, but build one that feels like a friend, not some funnel.

The marketers who master WhatsApp now will be the ones leading retention, LTV, and brand trust tomorrow.

So, if you're reading this, you're already ahead of the curve. And now in the Top 1% of Marketers who are already aware of **WhatsApp Marketing**.

Keep going. Keep testing. Keep the conversation rolling.

"The future of marketing isn't about **reach** — it's about response".

Author's Note

Hey {{*Your First Name*}} — thanks a million for reading my second book about WhatsApp Marketing strategy.

If you've made it this far, I just want to say I appreciate your time.

Seriously.

You didn't just skim — you cared enough to understand how WhatsApp is changing the game for digital marketers like us.

I wrote this book because I believe we're entering a new era where conversations, not campaigns, will drive growth. And I want more marketers — especially the sharp, curious, forward thinking ones like you — to get ahead of the curve *before* it becomes the norm.

So if you found this helpful, here's a small ask:

👉 **Share it.**

- With that colleague who's still clinging to email open rates.
- With your boss or client who keeps asking for "something new."

- With a friend who's building their D2C brand.

We rise faster when we learn together.

If this book shifted how you think about WhatsApp marketing or growth, I'd love to hear your feedback on the same platform where you found my book.

There you can also find my other books mentioned in the next page and see what I did there as well.

Onward and upward,

— **Aries Ram**

Other Books I Have Written With The Same Vibe

1) **How To Sell The EMC³ Way**

   A modern sales playbook for outreach that actually works. Learn how to Execute with precision, Message with clarity, Connect with empathy, and Convert consistently — no fluff, just practical strategies for digital-first selling.

2) **The SaaS Prescription: Is Your Product a Painkiller, Antibiotic, or Vitamin?**

   A must-read framework for SaaS founders, product marketers, and growth teams. Discover how to position your product for urgency, relevance, and retention — and finally stop guessing why users churn or ignore your offer.

3) The Updated WhatsApp Commerce Playbook For eCommerce Founders & Marketers

Your hands on ecommerce guide to turning WhatsApp into a sales, support, and loyalty machine. Packed with use cases, flows, and real-world campaign ideas to drive orders, engage customers, and grow smarter — all inside your customer's favorite app.

due diligence and consulting with professional advisors before making business or financial decisions.

The mention of any company, tool, or platform in this book is based on research and experience; however, no official endorsements are implied. WhatsApp is a registered trademark of Meta Platforms, Inc., and again, this book is not affiliated with, endorsed by, or sponsored by WhatsApp or Meta.

By reading this book, you acknowledge that the author and publisher are not responsible for any decisions you make based on its contents.

Disclaimer - The author and publisher are not affiliated with, endorsed by, or promoting any of the brand names, business names, WhatsApp marketing platforms, or CRM tools mentioned in this book. All trademarks, product names, company names, or logos cited herein are the property of their respective owners. References to these names are made purely for informational and illustrative purposes, and do not constitute an endorsement or recommendation.

If you choose to explore or use any of the tools or platforms mentioned, please contact the respective companies directly for the most accurate and up-to-date information.